TEACHers
Edition

30 pages

By Veronica Geng

Illustrated by Huntly Braun

called Guess who?

1980
Merry Christmas
Colette
from
John & Mary Jo
Thank you

A Cavalcade of Famous Americans

GUESS WHO?

A Cavalcade of Famous Americans

By Veronica Geng

Illustrated by
Huntley Brown

PLATT & MUNK, *Publishers* : NEW YORK

Guess Who? is a book about people who have made America the rich and varied country it is. Before you read about these people and see what they look like, you can have the fun of trying to guess who they are. First read the clues about the person, then, when you've made your guess, turn the page and see if you're right.

1. He was not poor, and his name was not Richard.

2. His picture is on a $100 bill.

3. He was a printer by trade, but he invented a stove, a harmonica, and a funny-looking pair of eyeglasses.

4. To prove an idea he had, he flew a kite in a thunderstorm.

1. He was born in England, but he helped the American colonies to rebel against England.

2. He felt that it was not common sense for a big country to be ruled by a faraway small country.

3. He expressed his views in books he printed himself.

4. His last name sounds like a word meaning "ache."

Benjamin Franklin   1706-1790

Ben Franklin is often called "the first American" for his knack of getting things done fast and well. To prove that lightning was electricity, for example, he flew a kite in a storm. At 17 he settled in Philadelphia and started his own printing business. Soon he was putting out a lively newspaper, as well as *Poor Richard's Almanac*—a mixture of calendars, advice to farmers, jokes, sayings, and stories. Franklin gave Philadelphia its first fire company, public library, university, and public hospital. He served in the Congress, helped write the Declaration of Independence and the Constitution, and became the first United States ambassador to France.

Thomas Paine   1737-1809

A bankrupt drifter, Tom Paine joined the many colonists seeking a fresh start in America, and arrived in Philadelphia in 1774. He became a printer, writing and publishing pamphlets on important issues. He wrote against slavery and in favor of democratic government. On January 10, 1776, Paine published his most famous pamphlet, *Common Sense*. In it, he urged the colonies to revolt against England immediately. A large country like America, he said in plain, strong words, should be free to govern itself. There was already a growing independence movement in the colonies, and *Common Sense* convinced many more people to support independence.

1. He designed and built a workable submarine, but he is more famous for another kind of boat.

2. He figured out how to use steam to power a boat.

3. His first steamboat was a failure.

4. His second steamboat made a successful trip up a river in New York.

1. He was an inventor.

2. He invented a machine that could send messages over long distances.

3. This invention was not the telephone.

4. He invented a code of dots and dashes that is named after him.

Robert Fulton   1765-1815

Fulton showed engineering talent as a boy, making fireworks and rifles that he designed himself. The first boats he built were experimental submarines. They worked, but they could not travel very fast. Fulton's next design was a steamboat. Steam engines had been used to drive trains, but no one had built a workable steamboat. Fulton's first steamboat sank. The engine was too heavy. Finally, in 1807, his steamboat *Clermont* made its first trip, from New York City to Albany, up the Hudson River. Soon steamboats were busily carrying passengers and goods up and down the nation's rivers.

Samuel F. B. Morse   1791-1872

One day Morse, a painter, was chatting with a fellow passenger on an ocean voyage. They talked of experiments with electricity. Could electric signals send a coded message over a long distance? Morse set out to invent electric machines to send and receive signals in code. Joseph Henry, a famous scientist, generously gave Morse many of his own ideas on electromagnetism, though Morse later denied that Henry had helped him. In 1843 Morse convinced Congress to spend $30,000 on a telegraph line between Baltimore and Washington. On May 24, 1844, Morse sent the first telegraph message: "What hath God wrought!"

1. His real name was John Chapman, but he is known by another name.
2. He lived in Ohio, but he traveled a great deal.
3. On his travels, he often planted trees.
4. He liked apples.

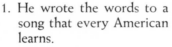

1. He wrote the words to a song that every American learns.
2. The song is played at the start of professional baseball games.
3. All Americans are supposed to stand when this song is played.
4. He wrote the words to the song while on a boat watching bombs bursting in the air over a fort.

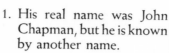

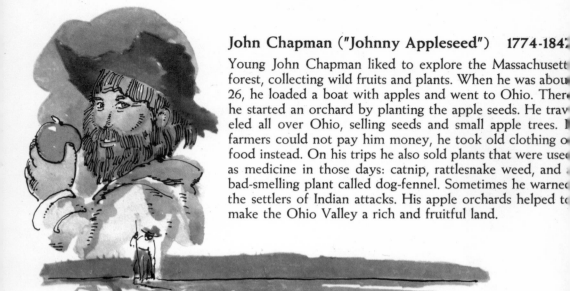

John Chapman ("Johnny Appleseed") 1774-184?

Young John Chapman liked to explore the Massachusett
forest, collecting wild fruits and plants. When he was abou
26, he loaded a boat with apples and went to Ohio. There
he started an orchard by planting the apple seeds. He trav
eled all over Ohio, selling seeds and small apple trees. I
farmers could not pay him money, he took old clothing o
food instead. On his trips he also sold plants that were use
as medicine in those days: catnip, rattlesnake weed, and
bad-smelling plant called dog-fennel. Sometimes he warned
the settlers of Indian attacks. His apple orchards helped to
make the Ohio Valley a rich and fruitful land.

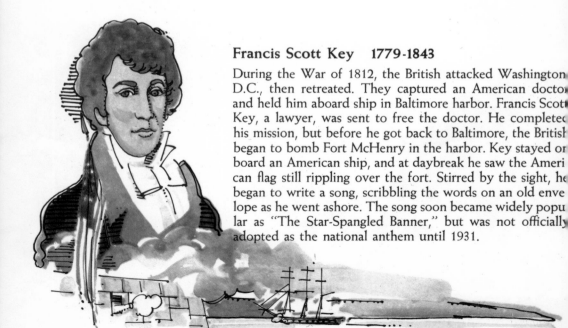

Francis Scott Key 1779-1843

During the War of 1812, the British attacked Washington
D.C., then retreated. They captured an American doctor
and held him aboard ship in Baltimore harbor. Francis Scott
Key, a lawyer, was sent to free the doctor. He completed
his mission, but before he got back to Baltimore, the British
began to bomb Fort McHenry in the harbor. Key stayed on
board an American ship, and at daybreak he saw the Ameri
can flag still rippling over the fort. Stirred by the sight, he
began to write a song, scribbling the words on an old enve
lope as he went ashore. The song soon became widely popu
lar as "The Star-Spangled Banner," but was not officially
adopted as the national anthem until 1931.

1. He served in the army commanded by George Washington.

2. He often wrote letters in code.

3. A British officer was hanged because he was captured with one of these letters hidden in his boot.

4. His name has come to mean "treason."

1. Her name means "playful one" in her Indian language.

2. She lived near the first English settlement in America.

3. She saved the life of this settlement's leader.

4. Her father was a chief named Powhatan.

Benedict Arnold 1741-1801

Arnold began his career as a brave, dedicated American soldier. During the American Revolution, he was promoted to brigadier general. But younger men were being promoted above him, and Arnold grew more and more bitter. He also needed money. Finally, in 1779, he sent a messenger to the British, offering to spy for the British army. Major John André, aide to the British general, accepted his offer. In 1780 Arnold became commander of the American fort at West Point, New York. He wrote to André, offering to surrender the fort. André was captured, and Arnold fled to the British lines. He went to England to live, but few people trusted him, and he died there in poverty and disgrace.

Pocahontas 1595 (?)-1617

Pocahontas, the daughter of Chief Powhatan, grew up near the English fort at Jamestown, Virginia. One day, Jamestown's leader, Captain John Smith, was captured by Indians. They were about to beat him to death, but Pocahontas stood between Smith and the Indians, saving his life. Several years later the English captured Pocahontas and held her hostage for English prisoners. A young Englishman, John Rolfe, fell in love with her. They were married at the church in Jamestown, and in 1616 sailed for England. There she met the king and queen, who treated her like the princess she was. Just before returning to Virginia, Pocahontas died of smallpox. She was buried in England.

1. He was one of the first captains in the U.S. Navy.

2. He named his most famous ship in honor of Benjamin Franklin's "Poor Richard."

3. Although he was born in the British Isles, he led America to a famous naval victory over the British.

4. Asked to surrender in a battle, he said, "I have not yet begun to fight."

1. He was a pathfinder during the early days of the United States.

2. One of the paths he found was a route through the mountains from Tennessee to Kentucky.

3. He was an excellent hunter, trapper, and Indian fighter.

4. He led groups of pioneers to Kentucky.

John Paul Jones   1747-1792

John Paul Jones was the first American naval hero. Bor[n] in Scotland, he ran away to sea when he was 12. During th[e] American Revolution he commanded the ship he calle[d] the *Bonhomme Richard* in honor of Benjamin Franklin, wh[o] had gotten the ship from France. On September 23, 1779 the *Bonhomme Richard* met a much larger British ship, th[e] *Serapis*. The enemy asked Jones to surrender. Jones's f[a]mous answer came: "I have not yet begun to fight." His shi[p] was sinking. But he lashed it to the *Serapis*, and fought th[e] British hand-to-hand. This victory helped the colonies co[n]trol the sea during the war.

Daniel Boone   1734-1820

Boone was the most famous of the pioneers who blaze[d] trails to the West. His grandfather had been one of th[e] Quaker settlers of Pennsylvania. As a boy, Boone learne[d] to hunt and trap. In talking to the Indians, he heard of [a] land called Kentucky, across the Appalachian Mountain[s.] In 1775 he led a group of pioneers across the mountains [to] Kentucky. They established a camp, and built a fort call[ed] Boonesboro on the Kentucky River. Boone was an expe[rt] rifleman, and he helped them defend their fort against Indi[an] attacks. He also helped many other groups of pioneers sett[le] the dangerous wilderness west of the Appalachians.

1. He selected the location of the city that is named after him.

2. He was the first President to have his picture on a postage stamp.

3. He was the only President who did not live in Washington, D.C.

4. He has been called: "First in war, first in peace, and first in the hearts of his countrymen."

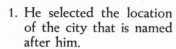

1. George Washington put him in charge of money matters for the new United States government.

2. He started the United States Mint.

3. His picture is on a $10 bill.

4. He was killed in a duel.

George Washington   1732-1799

As a young man, Washington served in the wars fought b[y]
England and the American colonies against the French an[d]
Indians. When the American Revolution broke out, Wash[-]
ington was named commander-in-chief of the coloni[al]
armies. He knew how to pick good generals, and he shape[d]
the disorganized colonial troops into a unified army. He le[d]
them through daring attacks on the British. And he inspire[d]
courage in them during the grim, icy winter they encampe[d]
at Valley Forge. After the war, as President, Washingto[n]
successfully created and unified a brand-new kind of gov[-]
ernment. He refused a third term of office, so that younge[r]
leaders could carry on his work.

Alexander Hamilton   1755 (1757?)-1804

When the United States government began, its leaders di[d]
not agree about its powers. Some said that the states shoul[d]
have the most power. Others said that the governmen[t]
could not work unless it had strong powers over the state[s]
Hamilton took the second view. And when he became th[e]
first Secretary of the Treasury, he followed this view i[n]
solving some of the money problems of his new countr[y]
He started import taxes to help pay the nation's debts. H[e]
started a national mint to coin money. That way, state[s]
could trade with each other without arguing over the valu[e]
of each state's money. Hamilton was killed in a duel wit[h]
one of his political rivals, Aaron Burr.

1. His friends called him Long Tom.

2. On the Fourth of July, Americans celebrate the signing of a document he wrote.

3. He spent $15 million to double the size of the United States.

4. He preferred life on his plantation to politics.

1. Thomas Jefferson sent these two men on an 8,000 mile trip.

2. On their journey, they had to take six tons of ammunition and supplies.

3. An Indian woman named Sacajawea served as their guide for part of the journey.

4. When they reached the ocean that Balboa discovered, they turned back.

WEST

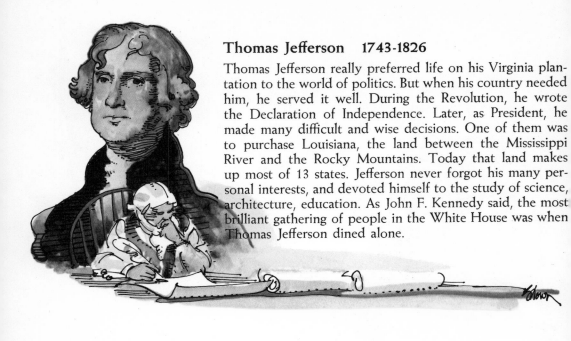

Thomas Jefferson   1743-1826

Thomas Jefferson really preferred life on his Virginia plantation to the world of politics. But when his country needed him, he served it well. During the Revolution, he wrote the Declaration of Independence. Later, as President, he made many difficult and wise decisions. One of them was to purchase Louisiana, the land between the Mississippi River and the Rocky Mountains. Today that land makes up most of 13 states. Jefferson never forgot his many personal interests, and devoted himself to the study of science, architecture, education. As John F. Kennedy said, the most brilliant gathering of people in the White House was when Thomas Jefferson dined alone.

Meriwether Lewis   1774-1809
William Clark   1770-1838

In 1803 Lieutenant William Clark got a letter from his friend Meriwether Lewis, President Jefferson's secretary. Jefferson was sending a party to explore the Louisiana Territory. Would Clark join? Clark did, and recruited 45 frontiersmen, including his Negro slave, York. An Indian woman, Sacajawea, guided them up the Missouri River and across the Rockies. Then they went beyond the Louisiana Territory, down the Columbia River in canoes, to the Pacific. They kept diaries describing the geography, minerals, wildlife, and Indians of the region. Clark drew maps and pictures of birds and animals. Their exploration helped to start a new era of trade in the West.

1. He invented the modern detective story.

2. He wrote a story about a bug.

3. He wrote a poem about a black bird.

4. His last name sounds like the name of a river in Italy.

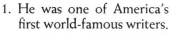

1. He was one of America's first world-famous writers.

2. He grew up near the river discovered by Henry Hudson.

3. He wrote a story about a young man who falls asleep and wakes up an old man.

4. One of his characters had no head.

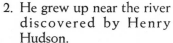

Edgar Allan Poe   1809-1849

Poe's life was marked by despair and loneliness. His father deserted the family and his mother died when he was two, so he was raised by foster parents, the Allans. Later, Poe lived with an aunt and her daughter, Virginia, whom he married. Poe worked as a magazine editor for $10 a week, but soon he was selling his stories and poems, including "The Raven." Then, in 1847, his young wife, Virginia, died. In poor health, Poe began drinking heavily, and tried to kill himself. One day he was found unconscious on a Baltimore street. He died soon afterward. Some of his most famous stories are "The Gold Bug," "The Pit and the Pendulum," and "The Purloined Letter."

Washington Irving   1783-1859

In the early years of the United States, many Europeans looked down on Americans as buckskin-wearing rubes who could barely scratch out their alphabet, let alone write good books. Irving helped to disprove this idea. He was a city man, not a frontiersman. He grew up in New York City, in a home full of books. He became a lawyer, and lived like a young man-about-town: gossiping in cafés, going to plays, writing essays and stories. Irving's most famous stories are "Rip Van Winkle" and "The Legend of Sleepy Hollow." In his last years, walking along the streets of New York, he was pointed out to visitors as "America's first writer."

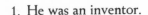

1. He was an inventor.

2. He invented a machine that lets people talk to each other over long distances.

3. The machine he invented is now in most homes in the United States.

4. His last name is a word meaning something that rings.

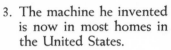

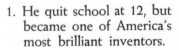

1. He quit school at 12, but became one of America's most brilliant inventors.

2. He figured out how to put motion pictures on a strip of film.

3. He invented the phonograph.

4. Without one of his inventions, people would have to use candles, gaslights, or oil lamps to see at night.

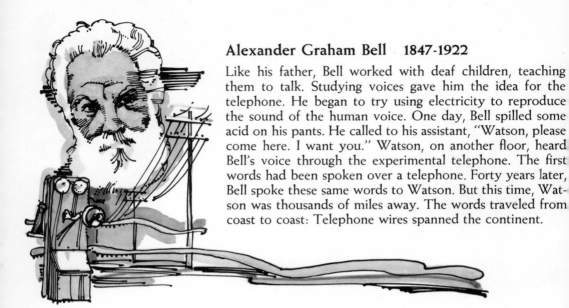

Alexander Graham Bell 1847-1922

Like his father, Bell worked with deaf children, teaching them to talk. Studying voices gave him the idea for the telephone. He began to try using electricity to reproduce the sound of the human voice. One day, Bell spilled some acid on his pants. He called to his assistant, "Watson, please come here. I want you." Watson, on another floor, heard Bell's voice through the experimental telephone. The first words had been spoken over a telephone. Forty years later, Bell spoke these same words to Watson. But this time, Watson was thousands of miles away. The words traveled from coast to coast: Telephone wires spanned the continent.

Thomas Alva Edison   1847-1931

Slow in school and poor at math, Edison quit school at 12 to work as a newsboy on a train. He used his wages to buy chemicals, for he loved experimenting. He even built a little lab in the baggage car on the train. Later he worked as a telegraph operator, and learned about electricity. By 1876, he had his own lab, and out of it poured a staggering series of inventions: a phonograph, a practical light bulb, a strip of motion picture film, and many others. By trial and error, sleepless nights, and tireless work, Edison became the most productive inventor of practical devices America has ever seen. He was also probably the only inventor who was as well-known to every American as the most famous movie star.

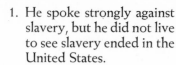

1. He spoke strongly against slavery, but he did not live to see slavery ended in the United States.

2. For two years he lived alone by a pond in Massachusetts.

3. He believed that a good citizen may sometimes refuse to pay taxes to the government.

4. He believed that men should try to lead simple lives, close to nature.

1. He was a French painter who moved to the United States.

2. He often killed wild birds, but he was not a hunter.

3. He liked to study and paint birds.

4. A society to protect wild birds is named after him.

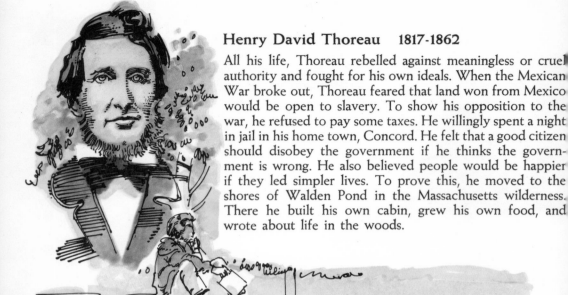

Henry David Thoreau   1817-1862

All his life, Thoreau rebelled against meaningless or cruel authority and fought for his own ideals. When the Mexican War broke out, Thoreau feared that land won from Mexico would be open to slavery. To show his opposition to the war, he refused to pay some taxes. He willingly spent a night in jail in his home town, Concord. He felt that a good citizen should disobey the government if he thinks the government is wrong. He also believed people would be happier if they led simpler lives. To prove this, he moved to the shores of Walden Pond in the Massachusetts wilderness. There he built his own cabin, grew his own food, and wrote about life in the woods.

John James Audubon   1785-1851

Audubon grew up in France. At 17, he went to study painting in Paris. Two years later, he went to America. He spent much time in the woods, looking for wild birds. First he studied a bird—its nest, its food, its way of walking and flying. Then he shot the bird and painted it in its natural setting. Audubon was the first in America to put a band on the foot of a bird so that he could free it and later recognize it in the woods; he wanted to study some birds without killing them. Other countries were curious about the strange wildlife of the New World. So Audubon's paintings grew popular all over the world, both for their beauty and for their scientific exactness.

1. She escaped from slavery by following the North Star.

2. She made hundreds of dangerous trips between the North and the South.

3. On these trips, she helped slaves to escape.

4. She worked as a spy during the Civil War.

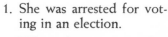

1. She was arrested for voting in an election.

2. When she gave speeches at meetings, she was often hissed and booed by men in the audience.

3. In 1920, 14 years after her death, her cause finally succeeded.

4. Among her best friends were Amelia Bloomer and Elizabeth Cady Stanton.

Harriet Tubman   1821 (?)-1913

Harriet Tubman grew up a slave, plowing fields and loading wood on a Maryland plantation. She escaped to the North, and decided to help others escape. With her rifle on her shoulder, she sneaked onto plantations and guided slaves to the North and into Canada. They traveled at night, and hid during the day at "stations"— homes of people who opposed slavery. This network of secret routes was called the Underground Railroad. Harriet Tubman led more than 300 slaves to freedom. When the Civil War started, she served as a scout and spy for the northern armies. After the war, she worked to start schools for the freed Negroes in the South.

Susan B. Anthony   1820-1906

Susan B. Anthony grew up in a Quaker family who believed that all people are equal. One day she went to an anti-slavery meeting and tried to give a speech. But the men shouted her down. In those days, ladies did not give speeches. In fact, women had few rights at all. Susan joined some other women in a campaign for women's rights, especially the right to vote. She even voted in an election, though she knew she would be promptly arrested. Susan B. Anthony died before winning her battle. But in 1920 her dream finally came true: for the first time, women of the United States could vote legally in an election.

1. He had visions in which he saw an angel.

2. He started a religion.

3. His followers were pioneers who helped settle the West.

4. Many people who belong to the religion he started live near a very salty lake.

1. He made a daring escape from slavery.

2. He worked on a "railroad" that did not have any trains or tracks.

3. He traveled to Britain to tell people about slavery in the United States.

4. He was one of the first workers for Negro civil rights.

Joseph Smith   1805-1884

Joseph Smith, who was born on a farm in New York State, founded the Church of Jesus Christ of Latter-Day Saints, often called the Mormon Church. From the time he was 15, he said, an angel appeared to him. The angel told him to start a new religion. In 1827 the angel led him to some golden plates buried in the ground. On them were written the Mormon teachings. Many people joined Smith's church. But others felt that the Mormons were strange, and did not welcome them. When Smith announced that Mormon men should have more than one wife, some non-Mormons arrested him and then killed him. Later, the Mormons settled the land that became the state of Utah.

Frederick Douglass   1817-1895

Douglass was born a slave on a Maryland plantation. When he was twenty, he escaped to the North disguised in a borrowed sailor's uniform, jumping on a train as it was pulling out of the station. In the North, he joined some abolitionists—people working against slavery. He helped them tell the public how cruel slavery really was. While on a tour of England, he heard that his master was looking for him. It was dangerous to go home. But he did—so he could help other slaves win freedom. In Rochester, New York, he headed an Underground Railroad station and printed an abolitionist newspaper. After the Civil War, Douglass worked for full civil rights for his people.

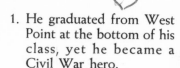

1. He graduated from West Point at the bottom of his class, yet he became a Civil War hero.

2. He helped defeat General Robert E. Lee.

3. Sitting Bull and Crazy Horse were two opponents he could not defeat.

4. The only survivor of his last stand in battle was a horse named Comanche.

1. His father, called Light-Horse Harry, served in the American Revolution under George Washington.

2. He ranked first in tactics in his class at West Point.

3. He rode a white horse named Traveller.

4. At a small farmhouse in Virginia, he surrendered to General U. S. Grant.

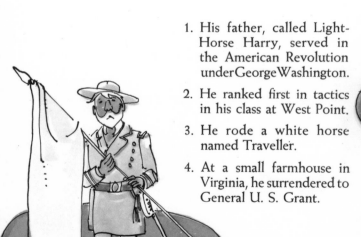

George Armstrong Custer   1839-1876

Custer was one of the most daring U.S. cavalry officers of the Civil War. In 1865 he defeated Lee at Richmond in a battle that helped force the South to surrender. After the war, the army sent Custer to fight the Sioux Indians, who refused to give up their land. Led by two great chiefs, Sitting Bull and Crazy Horse, thousands of Sioux encamped on the Little Bighorn River in Montana. Custer arrived nearby on the night of June 24, 1876. His orders told him to wait for reinforcements. But he learned that the Indians knew of his arrival. The next morning he led one-third of his 655-man force in an attack on the Indians' center. Custer and all the men under his command were killed.

Robert E. Lee   1807-1870

Born into a noted Virginia family, Lee attended West Point, ranking first in his class in artillery and tactics. He did not approve of slavery, and he did not want the South to separate from the Union. But when Lincoln offered him command of the Union Army, he resigned rather than fight against Virginia, his homeland. When the South fired on Fort Sumter, Lee took command of the southern forces in Virginia, and towards the end of the war he became commander of all the southern troops. Lee often outfought the enemy against great odds. On April 9, 1865, he surrendered to General Grant in a Virginia farmhouse. Looking toward the future, Lee asked that his men be allowed to keep their horses, "for the spring plowing."

1. He lived in a time when the South was rebuilding itself.

2. He was born a slave, but he became an adviser to Presidents and business-men.

3. He said the American Negroes should work hard to earn their rights.

4. On a deserted plantation near Tuskegee, Alabama, he started a school.

1. Her whole family worked against slavery in the years before the Civil War.

2. She wrote a book that was hated in the South and loved in the North.

3. It was the first American book with a black man for a hero.

4. One of the characters in this book was named Simon Legree.

Booker T. Washington 1856-1915

The years after the Civil War were hard for the newly
freed Negroes in the South. Most had no schooling and no
skills. Booker T. Washington had been born a slave. As a
boy, he had worked in a salt mine while teaching himself to
read. His neighbors saved money and sent him to a school.
Later, Washington started a school for free Negroes—Tuskegee Institute, in Alabama. The students built their own
school buildings as part of their education. Washington felt
that Negroes should learn carpentry, bricklaying, and farm-
ing, as well as reading and arithmetic. Equal rights, he said,
could wait. These ideas were easy for white people to
accept, and so Booker T. Washington helped his people
through some hard years.

Harriet Beecher Stowe 1811-1896

Harriet Beecher Stowe's father was a minister. When she
was 21, she went with him to Cincinnati, where he taught
at a college that was a center of the abolitionist movement.
Harriet also visited a Kentucky plantation, and saw the
slaves treated cruelly. Her brother told her about the slave
markets he had seen in New Orleans. Soon the whole
family was urging her to write a book against slavery. In
1851 she finished just such a book, *Uncle Tom's Cabin*,
about a slave who flees to freedom in Canada. Southerners
hated its author. But in the North, the author of *Uncle
Tom's Cabin* was a heroine who had showed many people
how evil slavery really was.

1. He was a wartime President.

2. He was the first President to wear a beard. He grew it when an 11-year-old girl wrote to him, suggesting that he would look better with a beard because his face was so thin.

3. His picture appears on the current U.S. penny.

4. His career took him from a log cabin to a white house.

1. At his wedding, his famous relative Teddy was the center of attention.

2. He was the first President to appear on television.

3. He is often called by his initials.

4. His wife and his Scottie dog Fala were almost as familiar to the public as he was.

Abraham Lincoln   1809-1865

When Lincoln became President, the nation was divide
into two sections—North against South, those again
slavery and those for it. Lincoln had learned about politi
in Illinois, where he served in the state congress and learne
to bargain and compromise. He hoped he could preve
war. But when southern troops fired on a northern for
Fort Sumter, he realized that a war was unavoidable. Li
coln's strong devotion to the Union cause helped the pe
ple to endure the hard war years. Before the Civil War ha
ended, he was shot by an assassin, John Wilkes Booth,
a theater in Washington, D.C.

Franklin Delano Roosevelt   1882-1945

F.D.R. led the United States through some of its harde
years—the Great Depression. When he took office as Pre
dent in 1933, the Depression was at its worst. Banks ha
closed. Many people had no food or homes. Farmers cou
not sell their crops. But Roosevelt told the people, "The on
thing we have to fear is fear itself." He promised a "new dea
and his Presidency became known as the New Deal. Roos
velt's Congress passed laws to provide jobs and money f
workers, the elderly, and the unemployed. When Roosev
died, a young congressman summed up the feelings of t
world: "He was the only person I ever knew—anywhere
who was never afraid."

1. He was the first President to ride in an automobile, and the first to ride in an airplane.

2. While he was President, the United States got the rights to build an important canal.

3. He was the youngest man ever to become President.

4. A kind of toy bear is named after him.

1. He was chief of an Indian tribe in Oregon.

2. His tribe's name means "pierced nose," because these Indians once wore ornaments in their noses.

3. He tried to leave the United States and go to Canada.

4. His father, also a chief, was called Old Joseph.

Theodore Roosevelt 1858-1919

A frail, sickly child, "Teddy" Roosevelt exercised his way to good health, and he grew up believing in "the strenuous life." In his early career, Roosevelt battled crime as police commissioner of New York City. During the Spanish-American War, he led a volunteer regiment called the Rough Riders. When McKinley was assassinated in 1901, Vice President Roosevelt became President. He believed the government should take strong action to protect the nation and its people. Under his leadership, the Panama Canal was built, and laws were passed to protect Americans from unsafe food and drugs, and to preserve the nation's great forests. Roosevelt loved excitement and action, and brought vigor and style to the Presidency.

Chief Joseph 1840 (?)-1904

The Nez Percé Indians lived in the Wallowa Valley in Oregon. In 1876 the government decided to open this land to white settlers and put the Indians on a reservation in Idaho. After a few battles with the army, Chief Joseph decided to move his people. In mid-winter, the Indians began a 1,000-mile march to Canada. Only 30 miles from Canada, the army caught them and forced them to surrender. Chief Joseph vowed never again to fight a war. "I am tired of fighting," he said. "It is cold and we have no blankets. The little children are freezing to death. My heart is sick and sad. I am tired." He spent the rest of his life working to educate Indian children.

1. He was the best-known criminal defense lawyer of his time.

2. He fought against the death penalty for crimes.

3. He opposed William Jennings Bryan at the Scopes "Monkey Trial."

4. Spencer Tracy played him in the movie *Inherit the Wind*.

1. He was one of the best public speakers in American politics.

2. He was prosecuting attorney and a star witness at the famous "Monkey Trial."

3. He ran for President three times, but never won.

4. In a poem about him, his last name is rhymed with "lion."

Clarence Darrow   1857-1938

Darrow educated himself largely by reading his way through his father's library. As a young country lawyer in Ohio, he kept up with new ideas by reading the latest books about crime and other social problems. He championed these new ideas in court. He defended John Scopes's right to teach evolution. He defended labor leaders who tried to organize their workers into unions. He fought against the death penalty for any crime. Darrow was convinced that one of the main causes of crime was poverty: "If every man, woman, and child in the world had a chance to make a decent, fair, honest living, there would be no jails and no lawyers and no courts."

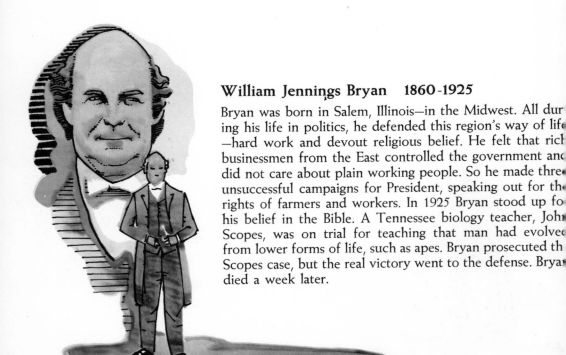

William Jennings Bryan   1860-1925

Bryan was born in Salem, Illinois—in the Midwest. All during his life in politics, he defended this region's way of life —hard work and devout religious belief. He felt that rich businessmen from the East controlled the government and did not care about plain working people. So he made three unsuccessful campaigns for President, speaking out for the rights of farmers and workers. In 1925 Bryan stood up for his belief in the Bible. A Tennessee biology teacher, John Scopes, was on trial for teaching that man had evolved from lower forms of life, such as apes. Bryan prosecuted the Scopes case, but the real victory went to the defense. Bryan died a week later.

1. Some people think he helped start a war between the United States and Spain.

2. He ran a New York newspaper that no longer exists.

3. This newspaper was the first to print color comics.

4. He lived in a castle in California.

1. She often appeared on Civil War battlefields, but she was not a soldier.

2. She was called Angel of the Battlefield.

3. Her real name was Clarissa, but she shortened it.

4. She started an American organization that has a red cross as its symbol.

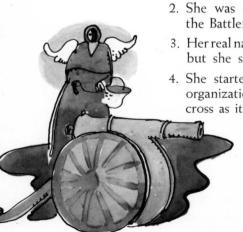

William Randolph Hearst   1863-1951

Hearst started a new look in newspapers when he bought
the *New York Journal*. He and Joseph Pulitzer, publisher
of the rival *New York World*, battled each other to attract
readers. Hearst published the first color comics and the first
Sunday magazine section. He ran huge headlines and exciting news of bloody crimes and scandals. In 1898 the
American battleship *Maine* was blown up off Cuba. The
Journal hinted that Spain had done it, though no one knew
for sure. The public desire for revenge, stirred up by the
Journal, was partly a cause of the war that followed. But
Hearst mostly cared about selling papers, and built a nation-
wide chain of newspapers that made him rich.

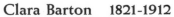

Clara Barton   1821-1912

When the Civil War started, Clara Barton heard of
wounded soldiers who had no medicine or food. She ad-
vertised in a newspaper, asking readers to send provisions.
Then she went straight to the battlefields, gave out the
provisions, and nursed the wounded. Soldiers were often
amazed to see a dark-haired little woman, only five feet
tall, crossing ditches and marching through the mud. After
the war, she set up an office to track down thousands of
soldiers reported missing in action. In 1869, on a trip to
Switzerland, she saw the work of the International Red
Cross. She started a branch in the United States, and became its first president.

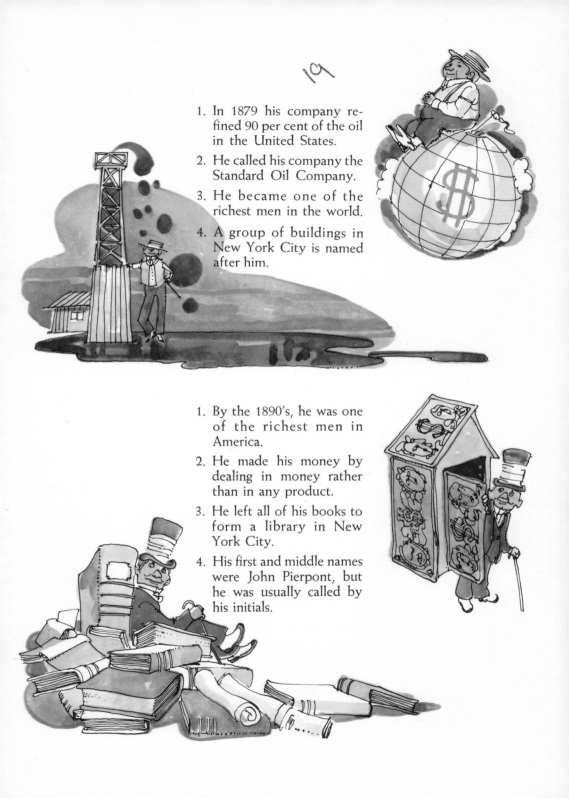

1. In 1879 his company refined 90 per cent of the oil in the United States.

2. He called his company the Standard Oil Company.

3. He became one of the richest men in the world.

4. A group of buildings in New York City is named after him.

1. By the 1890's, he was one of the richest men in America.

2. He made his money by dealing in money rather than in any product.

3. He left all of his books to form a library in New York City.

4. His first and middle names were John Pierpont, but he was usually called by his initials.

John D. Rockefeller   1839-1937

When Rockefeller finished high school, he looked for a job. "I was after something big," he said. His first job paid him only $3.50 a week. But by the time he was 38, he had built something very big indeed: the Standard Oil Company, which controlled the nation's entire oil industry. Rockefeller started out with one oil refinery. But he found ways to force rivals out of business. And his company made its own barrels and bought its own ships, so it did not have to pay for these services. Rockefeller left much of his fortune to start universities and to pay for medical and scientific research.

J. P. Morgan   1837-1913

One way to make money is to start a company that sells a product—like oil, or a service—like railroad transportation. Another way to make money is to lend money to these companies, and make a profit on the loan. J. P. Morgan was a master of the second way. His bank financed other banks, manufacturers, railroad companies, and even governments. Morgan wanted to make a profit, but he wanted to make it like a gentleman. He used his power honestly. And he often said he would never lend money to a man he didn't trust. He did not like being famous. In private, he collected rare books and paintings, which he left to start a library and a museum for the people of New York City.

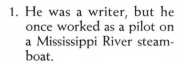

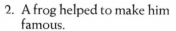

1. He was a writer, but he once worked as a pilot on a Mississippi River steamboat.

2. A frog helped to make him famous.

3. His boyhood friend Tom later became a character in a book he wrote.

4. His real name was Samuel Langhorne Clemens.

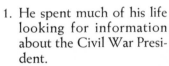

1. He spent much of his life looking for information about the Civil War President.

2. He wrote poems about the people of the biggest city in Illinois.

3. He was often seen strumming his guitar.

4. Part of his last name is a word for something you walk on at the beach.

Mark Twain   1835-1910

Twain grew up on the frontier, in a small town called Hannibal, Missouri. Hannibal is on the Mississippi River, and steamboats stopped there. As a young man, Twain learned to pilot a steamboat. On his trips he met all kinds of people who later went into his books: gamblers, eastern dudes, Negro slaves. His best book, and the one he loved most, was *The Adventures of Huckleberry Finn*. In it, a boy named Huck and a Negro slave named Jim float down the Mississippi on a raft—Jim to escape from slavery, Huck to escape from "sivilization." Like Huck, Twain could not stay in one place. He traveled all over the world, looking for people and places to write about.

Carl Sandburg   1878-1967

Sandburg wrote about "the people"— the plain people who settled the frontier and started the cities of America. He was one of them. He grew up on the Illinois prairie, working as a handyman, stagehand, wheat-harvester, newspaper man. Sandburg's first poem—"Chicago"—praised that rough, tough, meatpacking and railroad city. His life's work was a book about Lincoln. He went all over the country to find facts about Lincoln's life. On his travels, he read his poems and sang and played folk songs. Even as an old man, Sandburg got out among the people, playing his guitar, chatting about Lincoln and about Civil War history.

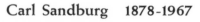

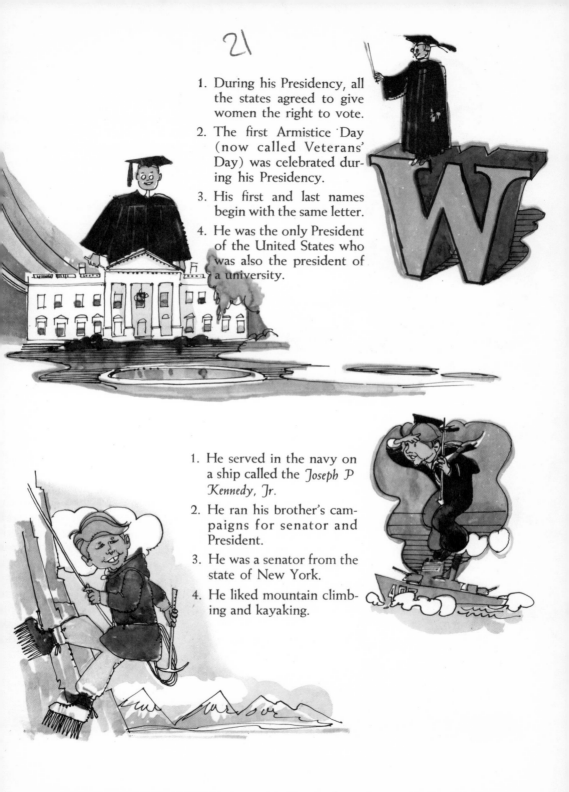

1. During his Presidency, all the states agreed to give women the right to vote.

2. The first Armistice Day (now called Veterans' Day) was celebrated during his Presidency.

3. His first and last names begin with the same letter.

4. He was the only President of the United States who was also the president of a university.

1. He served in the navy on a ship called the *Joseph P Kennedy, Jr.*

2. He ran his brother's campaigns for senator and President.

3. He was a senator from the state of New York.

4. He liked mountain climbing and kayaking.

Woodrow Wilson   1856-1924

When World War I began, President Wilson thought th
United States could play the strongest role by staying neu
tral, and acting as peacemaker. But in 1917, German sub
marines began sinking American ships. Wilson said war wa
necessary "to make the world safe for democracy." Afte
the war, Wilson suggested that the nations of the worl
form an organization where they could talk about thei
problems and work for peace. It was started and called th
League of Nations, but Wilson could not persuade th
Senate to approve United States membership in the Leagu
Today, the United Nations is based on Wilson's idea.

Robert Francis Kennedy   1925-1968

Robert Kennedy learned about politics as a young man, run
ning political campaigns for his brother John. He started hi
own career as a lawyer in the Department of Justice, and
later served as President John F. Kennedy's attorney gen
eral. In 1965 he became a senator from New York. An en
ergetic and curious man, Kennedy often took trips to se
for himself the problems of poor people in Appalachia, ir
the South, in the Negro ghettos of the cities, and on Indiar
reservations. He also worked hard to bring young peoplε
into politics. Kennedy was assassinated in California, whilε
campaigning there for the 1968 Presidential nomination

22

1. These two men were brothers.

2. They experimented with gliders before perfecting their most famous invention.

3. Without their invention, it would be possible to travel across an ocean only by boat.

4. Their first success came at Kitty Hawk, North Carolina.

1. He got a bonus of a hundred dollars every time he hit a home run. In 1927 he made $6,000 in these bonuses.

2. His lifetime record of 714 home runs still stands.

3. His real name was George Herman Ehrhardt.

4. Sportswriters called him the Sultan of Swat, the King of Clout, and the Bambino.

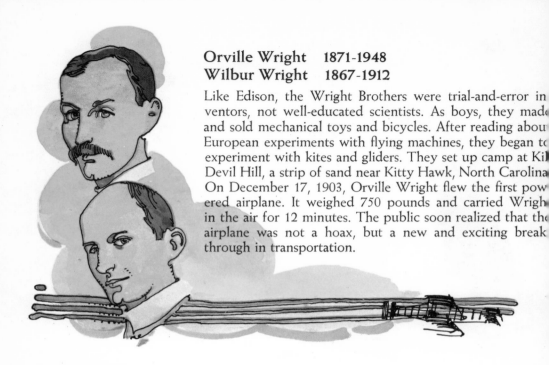

Orville Wright   1871-1948
Wilbur Wright   1867-1912

Like Edison, the Wright Brothers were trial-and-error inventors, not well-educated scientists. As boys, they made and sold mechanical toys and bicycles. After reading about European experiments with flying machines, they began to experiment with kites and gliders. They set up camp at Kill Devil Hill, a strip of sand near Kitty Hawk, North Carolina. On December 17, 1903, Orville Wright flew the first powered airplane. It weighed 750 pounds and carried Wright in the air for 12 minutes. The public soon realized that the airplane was not a hoax, but a new and exciting breakthrough in transportation.

Babe Ruth   1895-1948

In 1913 Jack Dunn, manager of the minor league Baltimore Orioles, signed an 18-year-old named George Herman Ruth. One of the Orioles' coaches said, "Well, here's Jack's newest Babe now!" From then on, Ruth was "the Babe." Ruth was an excellent pitcher and outfielder, but he became famous as the greatest home-run hitter of all time. As a member of the New York Yankees, he played on eight All-Star teams and led the American League in home runs for 12 seasons. Fans loved Ruth's shownmanship. During the 1932 World Series against the Chicago Cubs, he swung at two pitches, missed, then pointed to the centerfield flagpole. He hit the third pitch, and it sailed out of the park, right over the flagpole.

23

1. He started a museum that was like a circus sideshow.
2. He started "The Greatest Show on Earth."
3. This show featured a famous elephant.
4. His first and middle names were Phineas Taylor, but he was called by his initials.

1. He started out in life as a cowboy.
2. By 1934 he was the best-paid entertainer in the United States.
3. He never finished school, and he liked to say, "All I know is what I read in the papers."
4. His main skill was roping, but he was more famous for his jokes.

P. T. Barnum   1810-1891

Barnum was one of the first geniuses of advertising. He plastered towns with colorful posters about his shows. "There's a sucker born every minute," he said, as he charged people money to see such spectacles as an old lady who claimed to have been George Washington's nurse, a dwarf named General Tom Thumb, a bearded lady, and the first live hippopotamus seen in New York. Barnum started his famous circus, "The Greatest Show on Earth," in 1871. For years its main attraction was Jumbo the elephant, billed as the last surviving prehistoric mammoth. Like many of Barnum's claims, this was untrue. But no one seemed to mind.

Will Rogers   1879-1935

In 1905, a cowboy rope-artist appearing in a New York theater announced the tricks he was going to do. The audience laughed at what he said. He went on to joke with the audience. In this accidental way, Will Rogers suddenly became a success as a performer. Born on an Oklahoma ranch, Rogers worked as a cowboy, then joined a circus as a roper and rough-rider. After his New York success, he made screen and stage appearances and wrote a newspaper column. "I just played my natchell self," he always insisted. Posing as a simple cowboy philosopher, he poked fun at wars, Presidents, and politics. But behind his big innocent grin, he was criticizing what he thought was silly or wrong in the world.

24

1. He played basketball at Overbrook High School in Philadelphia.

2. In the 1959-1960 season, he was named the Most Valuable Player in the National Basketball Association.

3. He was a two-time All-American at the University of Kansas.

4. When he played for the Philadelphia Warriors, he was seven feet tall.

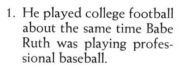

1. He played college football about the same time Babe Ruth was playing professional baseball.

2. He had bright red hair that gave him one of his nicknames.

3. One of his other nicknames was the Galloping Ghost.

4. He played for the University of Illinois.

Wilt Chamberlain   1936-

At 14, Wilt Chamberlain suddenly began to grow, fast. One
summer he grew four inches. By the time he entered Overbrook High School in Philadelphia, he was six feet eleven
inches tall and a star basketball player. At the University of
Kansas, which he attended for three years, he scored 52
points in his first varsity basketball game as a sophomore.
Kansas won 42 out of the 50 games in which Chamberlain
played. He averaged 30 points per game in his two varsity
seasons. Chamberlain joined the Harlem Globetrotters, then
went on to play with the Philadelphia Warriors. His seven
foot height won him the name "Wilt the Stilt."

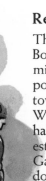

Red Grange   1903-

The 1920's were the Golden Age of Sports. Baseball had Ruth
Boxing had Dempsey. And college football had a red-headed
miracle named Harold E. Grange. Grange developed his
powerful leg and shoulder muscles delivering ice in his home
town, Wheaton, Illinois. At the University of Illinois, "the
Wheaton Iceman" was a three-time All-American, playing
halfback and quarterback. Grange was probably the greatest ball-carrier of all time. In a typical performance, "the
Galloping Ghost" gained 303 yards and scored four touch-
downs in 12 minutes. Said his unbelieving opponents, "All
that guy can do is run."

25

1. He was once an airmail pilot.
2. He won $25,000 for flying from New York to Paris.
3. He was the only person in the plane when he made his flight.
4. The flight took over five times as long then as it does today.

1. For a while, he worked as a navy test pilot.
2. He took a trip in *Freedom 7*.
3. He traveled 117 miles into space.
4. He was the United States' first man in space.

Charles A. Lindbergh   1902-

Lindbergh quit college to go to flight school. Then he bought a plane that had been used in World War I, and made "barnstorming" tours—demonstrations of trick flying—all over the Midwest. Later the government hired him to fly mail from St. Louis to Chicago. In 1927 he decided to compete for a prize of $25,000 offered for the first nonstop solo flight from New York to Paris. On the rainy morning of May 20, he took off from Long Island, New York, alone in his single-engine plane, the *Spirit of St. Louis.* After 33½ hours of flight in stormy weather, his plane touched down at Le Bourget, an airfield just outside Paris. Only 25 years old, he became a hero to the whole world.

Alan B. Shepard, Jr.   1923-

In 1959, the first seven American astronauts were picked. One of them was Commander Alan Shepard. He had graduated from the Naval Academy, served on a destroyer in World War II, and tested jets for the navy. After intense training, he was chosen to be the first American in space. On May 5, 1961, at Cape Canaveral (now Cape Kennedy), Florida, Shepard's space capsule *Freedom* 7, mounted on a rocket, blasted off into space. At about 243,640 feet, the capsule separated from the rocket, and Shepard took the controls, moving the capsule in orbit around the earth. The United States had sent its first pioneer to explore a new frontier—outer space.

1. He grew up in New Orleans when that city was the jazz center of the world.
2. His teacher was Joe "King" Oliver.
3. He plays the trumpet.
4. He is famous for his deep, rasping voice.

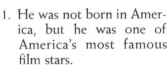

1. He was not born in America, but he was one of America's most famous film stars.
2. He made many films in which he did not speak a single word.
3. He was a comedian, and was very good at falling down while roller-skating.
4. He often wore a small black mustache.

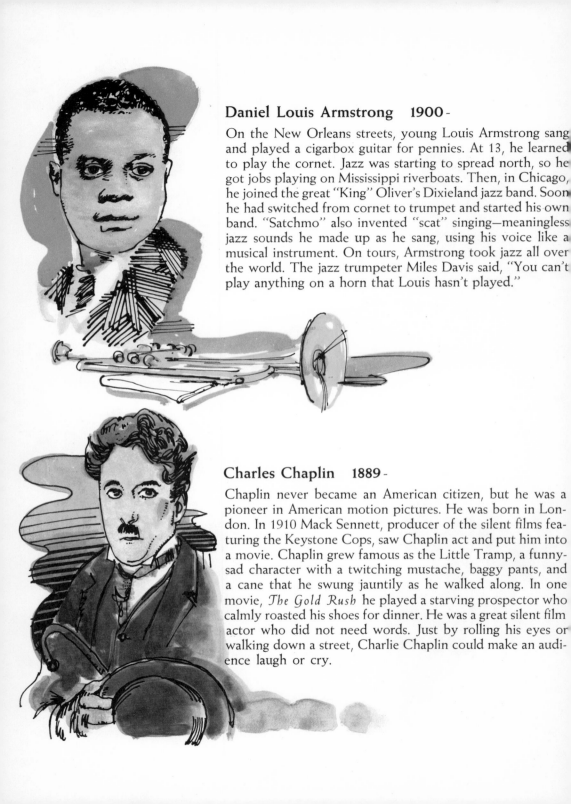

Daniel Louis Armstrong   1900-

On the New Orleans streets, young Louis Armstrong sang and played a cigarbox guitar for pennies. At 13, he learned to play the cornet. Jazz was starting to spread north, so he got jobs playing on Mississippi riverboats. Then, in Chicago, he joined the great "King" Oliver's Dixieland jazz band. Soon he had switched from cornet to trumpet and started his own band. "Satchmo" also invented "scat" singing—meaningless jazz sounds he made up as he sang, using his voice like a musical instrument. On tours, Armstrong took jazz all over the world. The jazz trumpeter Miles Davis said, "You can't play anything on a horn that Louis hasn't played."

Charles Chaplin   1889-

Chaplin never became an American citizen, but he was a pioneer in American motion pictures. He was born in London. In 1910 Mack Sennett, producer of the silent films featuring the Keystone Cops, saw Chaplin act and put him into a movie. Chaplin grew famous as the Little Tramp, a funny-sad character with a twitching mustache, baggy pants, and a cane that he swung jauntily as he walked along. In one movie, *The Gold Rush* he played a starving prospector who calmly roasted his shoes for dinner. He was a great silent film actor who did not need words. Just by rolling his eyes or walking down a street, Charlie Chaplin could make an audience laugh or cry.

1. He was one of New York City's most popular mayors.

2. He battled "Gentleman" Jimmy Walker for the election.

3. A New York airport is named after him.

4. His first name means "little flower" in Italian, and he was often called the Little Flower as a nickname.

1. It was not safe to drink liquor in a saloon if she was in the neighborhood.

2. Her trademark was a hatchet.

3. She caused thousands of dollars worth of damage in cities from coast to coast.

4. She convinced many people that drinking liquor was a sin.

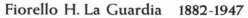

Fiorello H. La Guardia 1882-1947

The mayor of New York City has one of the toughest jobs in the nation. La Guardia was one of the best and most popular mayors of this huge city. He started in politics in the House of Representatives, where he made a splash by pulling a roast beef out of his pocket: "What workingman's family can afford to pay $3.00 for a roast of this size?" In 1933 he ran for mayor against the debonair Mayor Jimmy Walker. To appeal to voters, La Guardia gave speeches in Yiddish and Italian. He promised to use city money to help the people. As mayor, he cut his own salary to get money for schools, parks, and bridges. During a newspaper strike, he read the Sunday comics to children over the radio.

Carry Nation 1846-1911

Carry Nation thought drinking liquor was sinful. And in Kansas, where she lived, it was illegal. She was a strong woman, nearly six feet tall. She forced her way into saloons and smashed everything in sight—windows, furniture, mirrors, paintings, and, of course, bottles of liquor. Saloon property, she said, "has no rights that anyone is bound to respect." She first used a hatchet to tear a saloon apart in Wichita, and went on to attack saloons from San Francisco to New York. When she was arrested, she paid her fine by selling toy hatchets and giving lecture tours. She also gave much of her money to the poor, and started a home for drunkards' wives.

28

1. After his first season in the American League, his batting average never fell below .300.

2. Born in Georgia, his nickname was the Georgia Peach.

3. He retired from baseball in 1928.

4. He played more seasons as a major league regular than any player before or since.

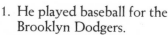

1. He played baseball for the Brooklyn Dodgers.

2. He was a high school and college star in football, basketball, and track, as well as baseball.

3. In his first season with the Dodgers, they won the National League pennant.

4. He was the first Negro to play in modern-day professional, organized baseball.

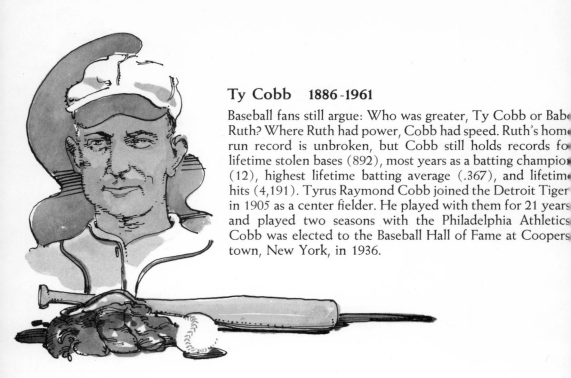

Ty Cobb 1886-1961

Baseball fans still argue: Who was greater, Ty Cobb or Babe Ruth? Where Ruth had power, Cobb had speed. Ruth's home run record is unbroken, but Cobb still holds records for lifetime stolen bases (892), most years as a batting champion (12), highest lifetime batting average (.367), and lifetime hits (4,191). Tyrus Raymond Cobb joined the Detroit Tigers in 1905 as a center fielder. He played with them for 21 years and played two seasons with the Philadelphia Athletics. Cobb was elected to the Baseball Hall of Fame at Coopers town, New York, in 1936.

Jackie Robinson 1919-

In high school and college sports, Jackie Robinson was good at everything. On an athletic scholarship at UCLA, he played football and won the National Collegiate broad jump title. But he came to national attention when the Brooklyn Dodgers signed him in 1947. For 70 years, professional baseball had been segregated. Robinson was the first Negro player to break this racial barrier. He proved himself brilliantly. He delighted crowds with his flashy base-running. And in ten seasons, his career batting average of .311 helped the Dodgers win six pennants and a World Series. In 1962 he was elected to the Baseball Hall of Fame.

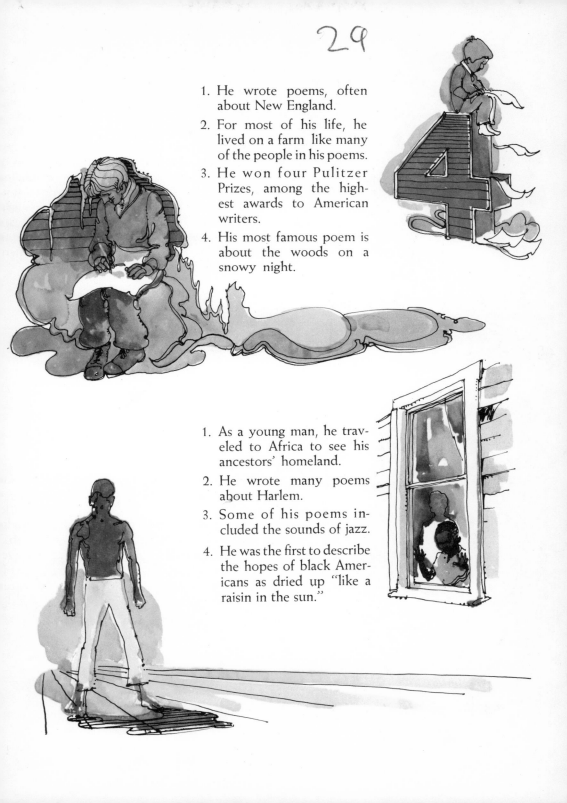

29

1. He wrote poems, often about New England.
2. For most of his life, he lived on a farm like many of the people in his poems.
3. He won four Pulitzer Prizes, among the highest awards to American writers.
4. His most famous poem is about the woods on a snowy night.

1. As a young man, he traveled to Africa to see his ancestors' homeland.
2. He wrote many poems about Harlem.
3. Some of his poems included the sounds of jazz.
4. He was the first to describe the hopes of black Americans as dried up "like a raisin in the sun."

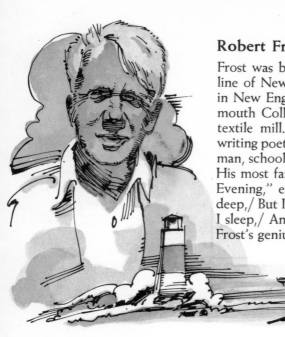

Robert Frost   1874-1963

Frost was born in San Francisco. But he came from a long line of New Hampshire Yankees, and lived most of his life in New England. Frost finished high school, but quit Dartmouth College after a few months and went to work in a textile mill. Like many poets who cannot make a living writing poetry, Frost had many jobs—shoemaker, newspaperman, schoolteacher, farmer. Frost's poems seem very simple. His most famous poem, "Stopping by Woods on a Sunday Evening," ends like this: "The woods are lovely, dark and deep,/ But I have promises to keep,/ And miles to go before I sleep,/ And miles to go before I sleep." This simplicity is Frost's genius for saying a lot in a few words.

Langston Hughes   1902-1967

Hughes grew up in the Midwest. His father, angry at the treatment of Negroes in America, had moved to Mexico. His mother worked, and Hughes lived with his grandmother. After graduating from high school, he worked his way to Africa on a freighter, to learn something about the land of his ancestors. On his return he took a job as a hotel busboy. He was discovered when he put three of his poems under the plate of a famous poet who dined at the hotel. He wrote poems about the slums and jazz clubs of Harlem, the cotton fields of the South. He wrote about the suffering and pride of black Americans. "I am the darker brother," he wrote, "I, too, am America."

30

1. He was the first Presidential candidate to debate his opponent on television.

2. In 1961 he gave the first live television press conference.

3. His great-grandfather came from Ireland to the United States as a poor immigrant. But the family soon produced a mayor of Boston and an ambassador to Britain.

4. He gave away PT-109 tie-clasps.

1. In a famous speech in 1965, he said, "I have a dream."

2. He helped start a revolution, but he did not believe in war or violence.

3. For one whole year, while he lived in Montgomery, Alabama, he did not ride the bus.

4. His last name is the same as the title given to royal rulers of countries.

John Fitzgerald Kennedy   1917-1963

During World War II, Kennedy served in the navy, commanding a torpedo boat called PT-109. He won a medal for his brave rescue of three of his men when the Japanese sank his boat. Later he was elected senator from Massachusetts and, in 1960, President. In his inauguration speech Kennedy called on all Americans to build a better nation "Ask not what your country can do for you—ask what you can do for your country." His ideals and his youth attracted many young people to serve in the government at home and in the Peace Corps. In 1963, he was shot and killed in Dallas, Texas. He was mourned by the whole world, as much for what he might have done as for what he did.

Martin Luther King, Jr.   1929-1968

In 1956, a 26-year-old Baptist minister led the Negroes of Montgomery, Alabama, in a protest against segregated buses. Shortly after, the Supreme Court ruled that segregated buses were unlawful. Martin Luther King had won his first victory for civil rights. His leadership was so successful that people began to speak of a "civil rights revolution." He organized peaceful marches to show that Negroes wanted freedom, right away, but without fighting or bitterness. In April 1968, he was shot and killed in Memphis, Tennessee. Rich and poor, great leaders and plain citizens, came to the funeral of the man who had been against violence and for "the weapon of love."